(my name)

loves to ________________

________________.

This is a drawing of what I love to do.

My progress chart

As you complete each page, find the letter here. Trace the letter and draw a picture.

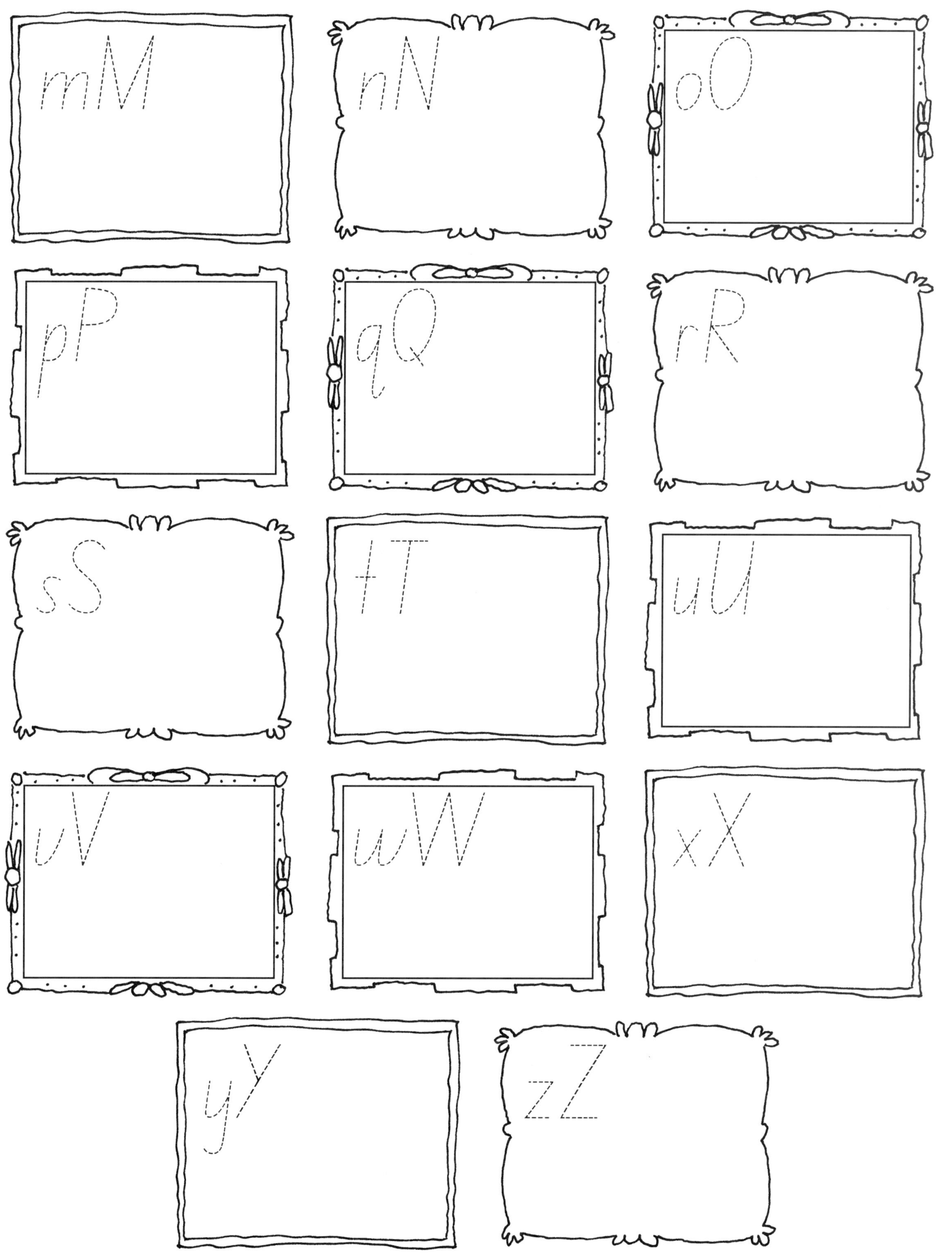
mM
nN
oO
pP
qQ
rR
sS
tT
uU
vV
wW
xX
yY
zZ

Continue the patterns. Keep your pencil on the page.

Copy the picture.

Handwriting: anticlockwise ellipse practice for letters a c C d e f g G o O q Q s S u U v w y

Continue the patterns. Keep your pencil on the page.

Copy the patterns.

Handwriting: clockwise ellipse practice for letters b B D h k m n p P r R

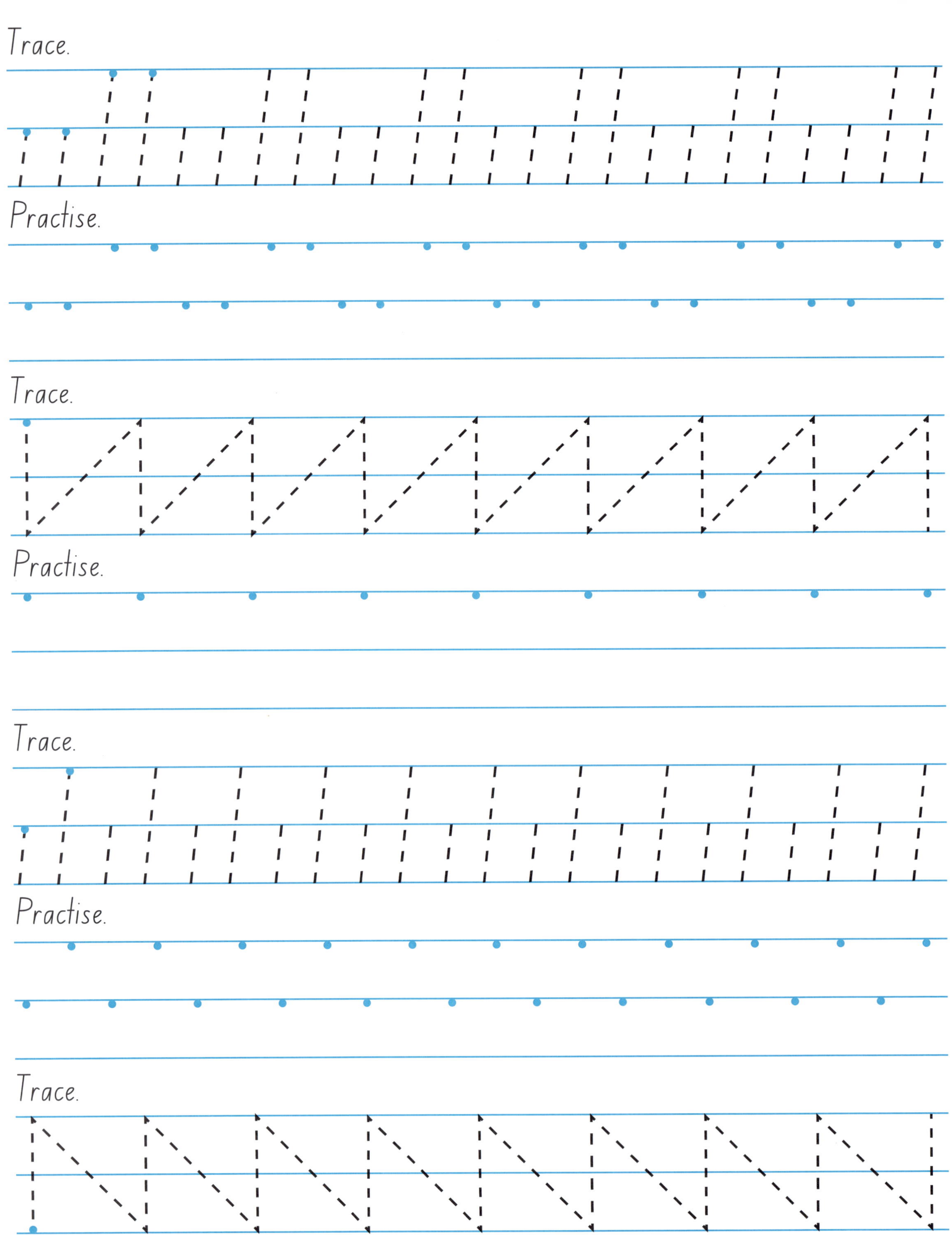

Handwriting: downward diagonal stroke practice for letters A E F H i l j J K l L M N t T V W x X Y z Z

Copy the patterns. Start at the dots.

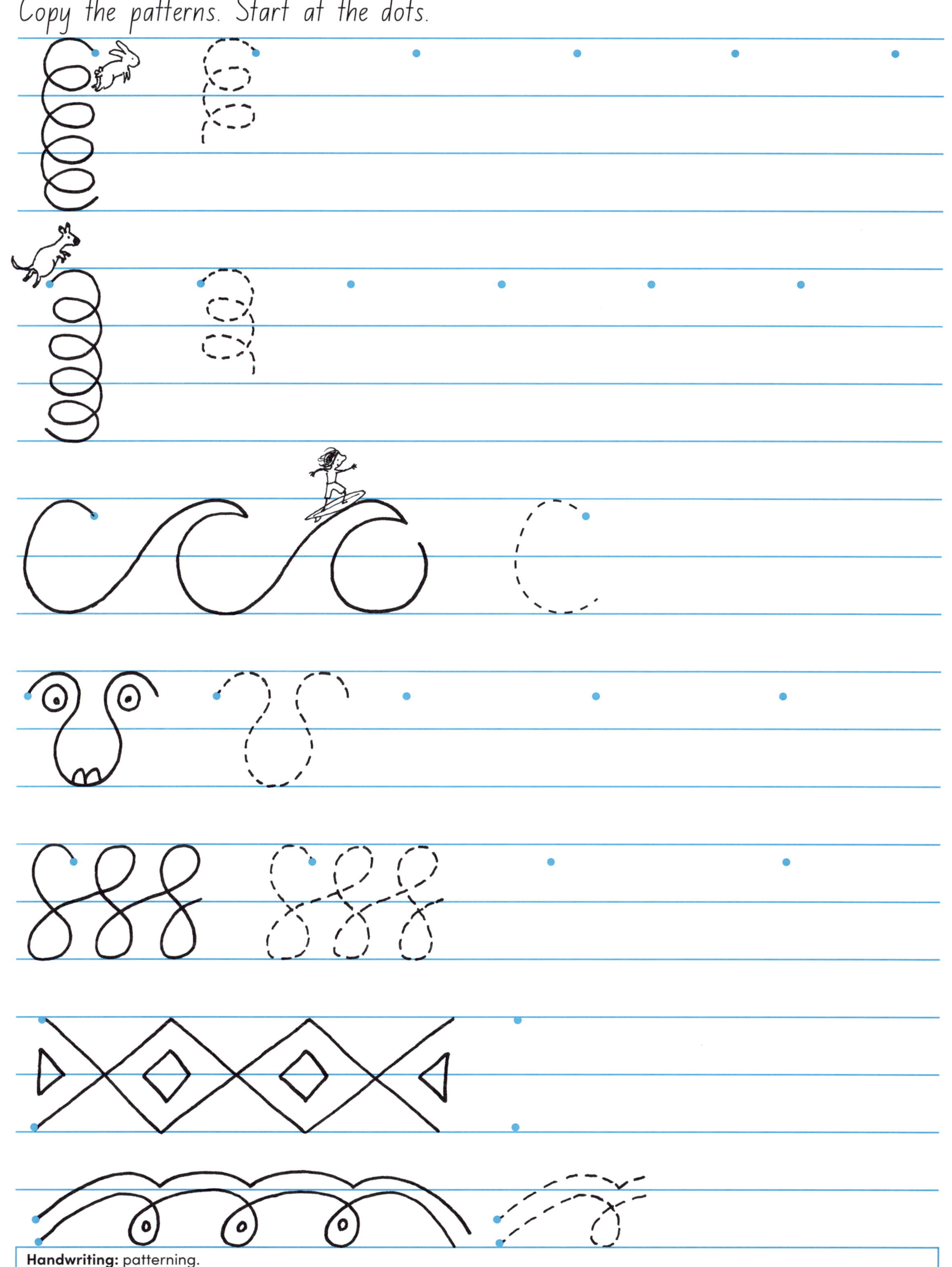

Handwriting: patterning.

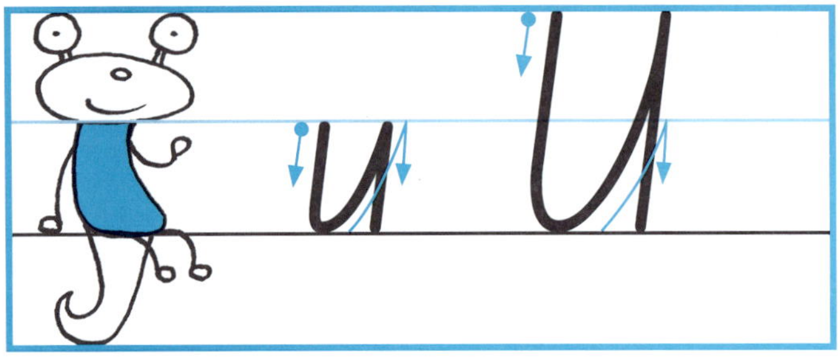

u U

Warm up.

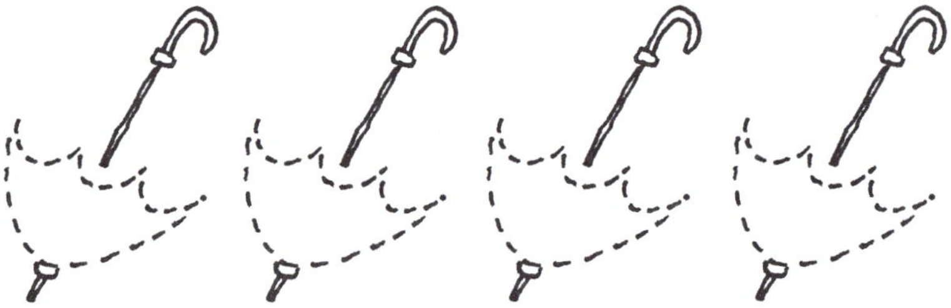

Track.

u u u u u u u u

Trace then write.

u u u u u u u u

u

Trace then write.

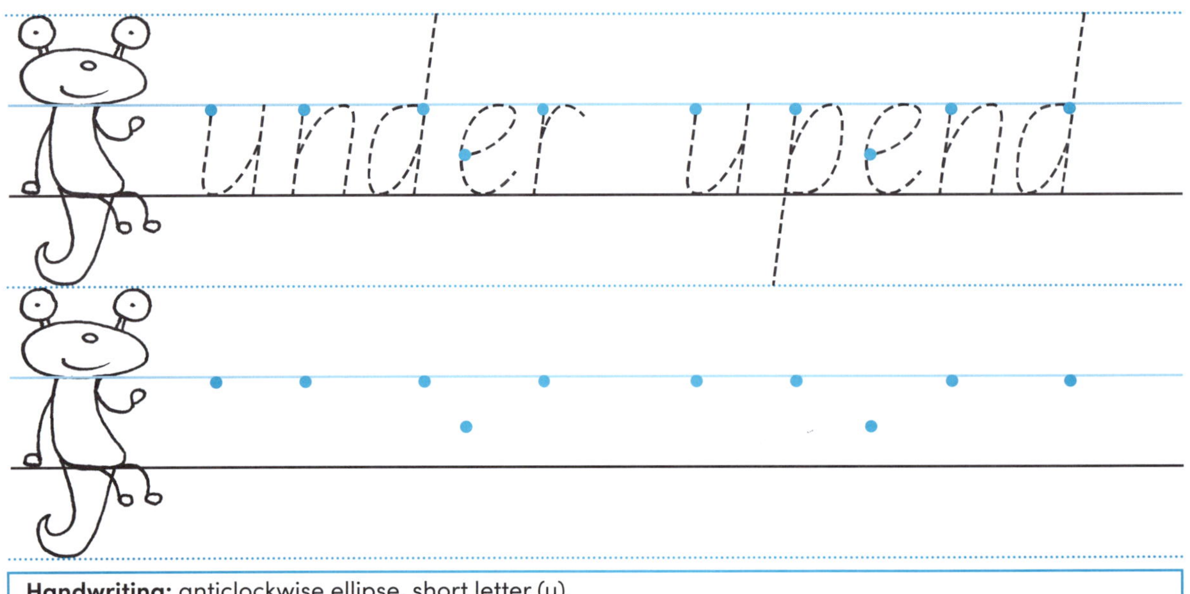

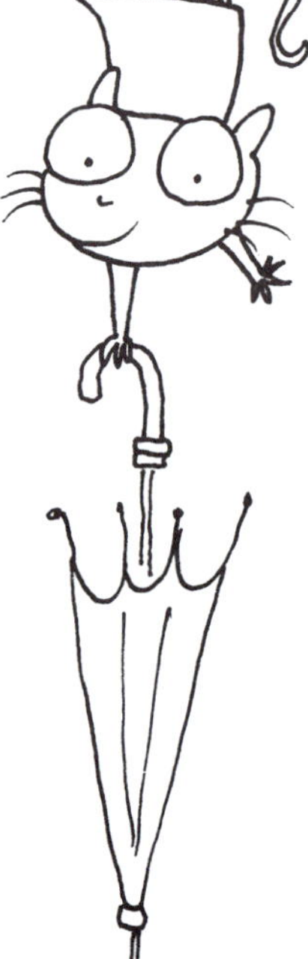

Handwriting: anticlockwise ellipse, short letter (u).
Grammar: saying verb (uttered), proper nouns (Uncle Uno).
Punctuation: sentence punctuation, exclamation mark, quotation marks.
Spelling and vocabulary: prefix un- (undo, untie, unzip), uncle, under, until, up, upend, upon, umbrella.
Literary elements: alliteration, onomatopoeia (ouch).

Trace then write.

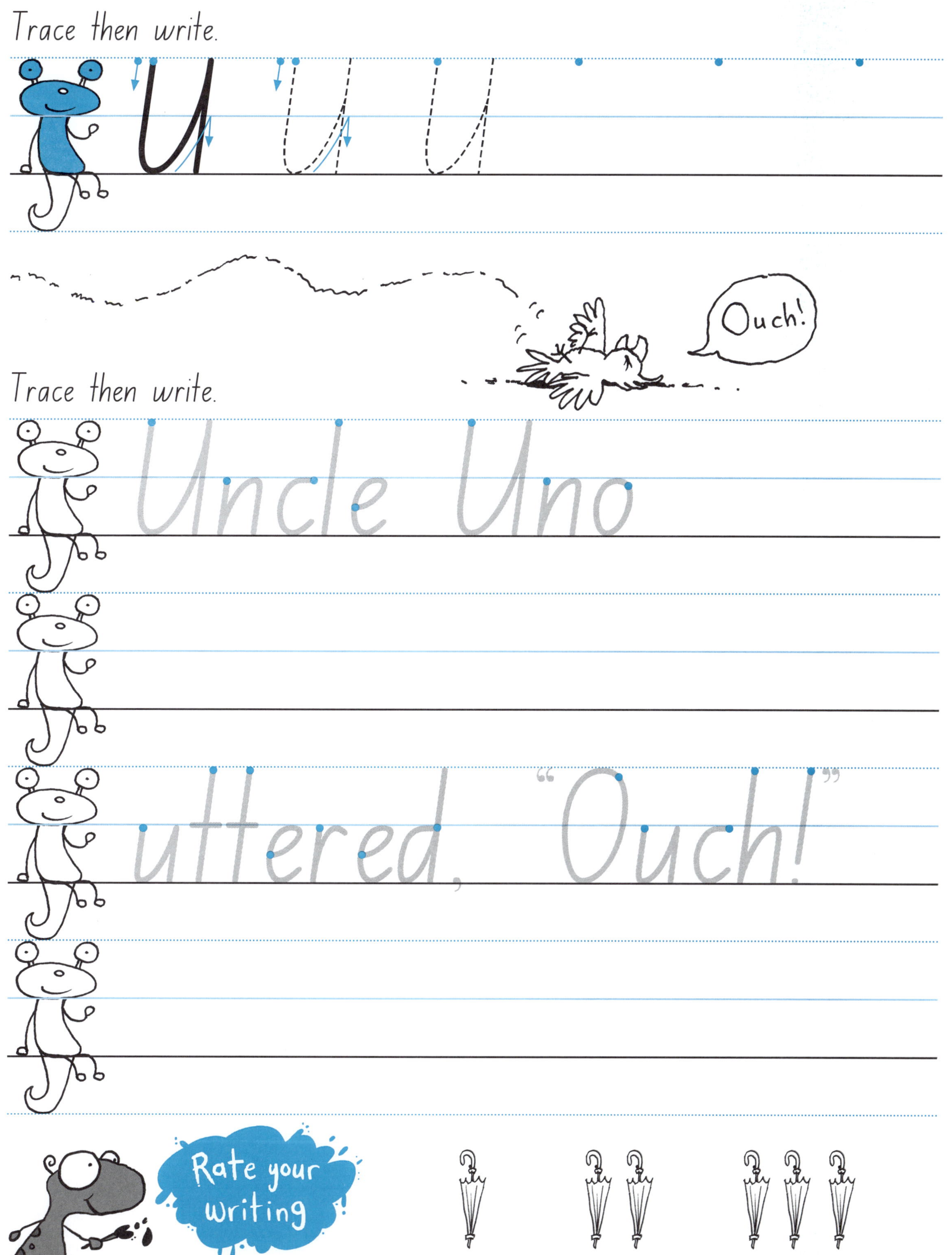

Trace then write.

Uncle Uno

uttered, "Ouch!"

Rate your writing

y Y

Warm up.

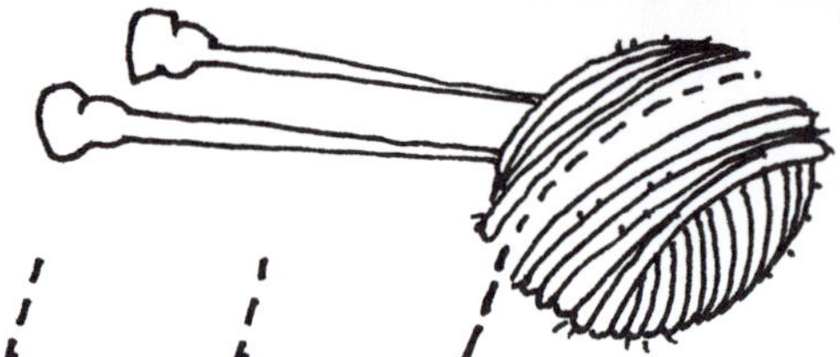

Track.

y y y y y y y

Trace then write.

y y y y y y y y

y

Trace then write.

year yawn yes

Handwriting: anticlockwise ellipse, long letter (y).
Grammar: saying verb (yak).
Punctuation: upper-case letter to start a sentence, full stop, speech bubble.
Spelling and vocabulary: yacht, yak, yap, yard, yarn, yawn, year, yen, yep, yes, yeti, yoga, yolk, you, yuan, yummy.
Literary elements: alliteration, onomatopoeia (yakkity yak), anthropomorphism.

Trace then write.

y y y

Trace then write.

Yaks yak on

yoga mats.

Rate your writing

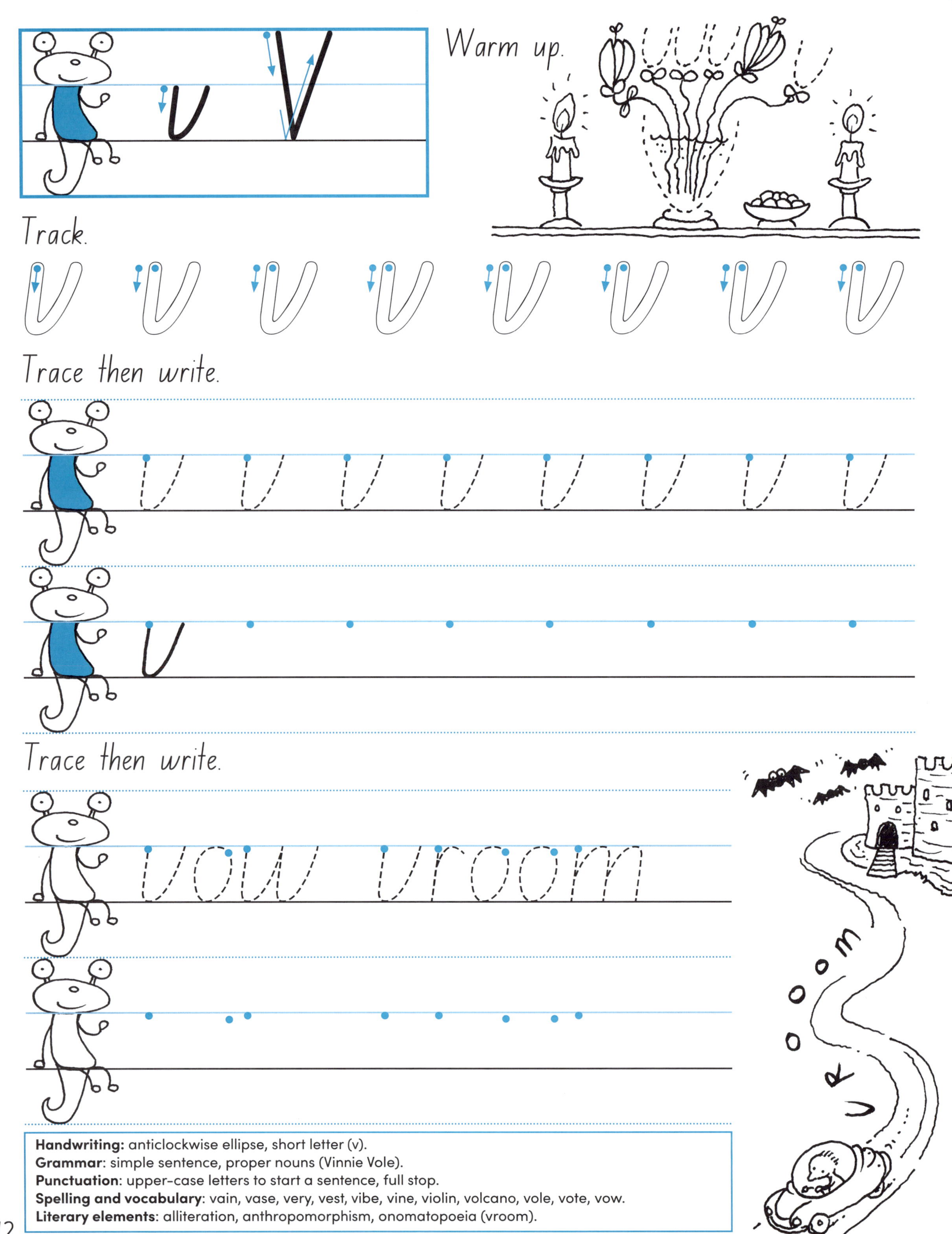

Handwriting: anticlockwise ellipse, short letter (v).
Grammar: simple sentence, proper nouns (Vinnie Vole).
Punctuation: upper-case letters to start a sentence, full stop.
Spelling and vocabulary: vain, vase, very, vest, vibe, vine, violin, volcano, vole, vote, vow.
Literary elements: alliteration, anthropomorphism, onomatopoeia (vroom).

Trace then write.

V V V

Trace then write.

Vinnie Vole

was very vain.

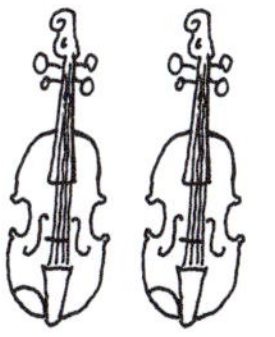

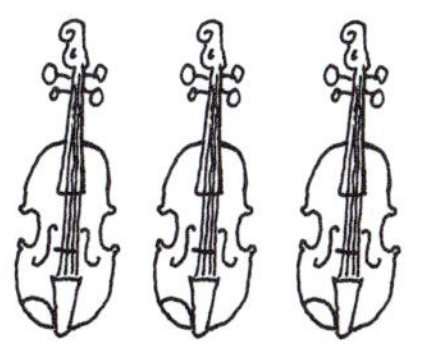

Handwriting: anticlockwise ellipse, short letter (w).
Grammar: saying verb (asked), proper noun (Wally), question.
Punctuation: upper-case letters to start a sentence, quotation marks, quoted speech, question mark.
Spelling and vocabulary: wall, walrus, watermelon, was, wasp, wave, Wednesday, when, whew, which, whiz, who, wild, wilt, win, wink.
Literary elements: alliteration, anthropomorphism.

Trace then write.

W W W

Trace then write.

"Who will win?"

asked Wally.

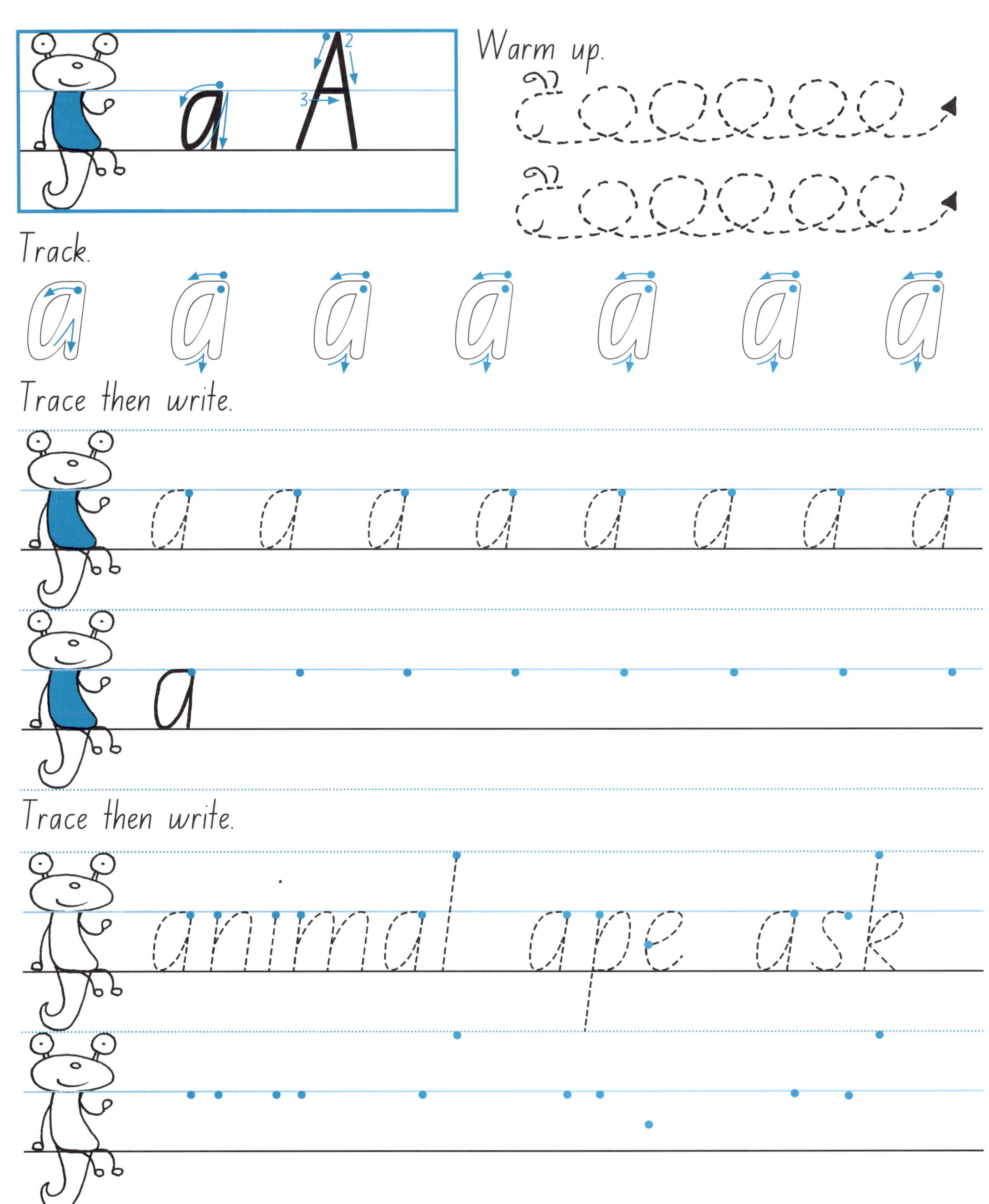

Handwriting: anticlockwise ellipse, short letter (a).
Grammar: simple sentence, action verb (ate).
Punctuation: upper-case letters to start a sentence, full stop.
Spelling and vocabulary: act, again, ago, all, allow, animal, any, ape, apple, April, arm, arrow, ash, ask, ate, August.
Literary elements: alliteration.

Trace then write.

A A A

Trace then write.

An anaconda

ate the apples.

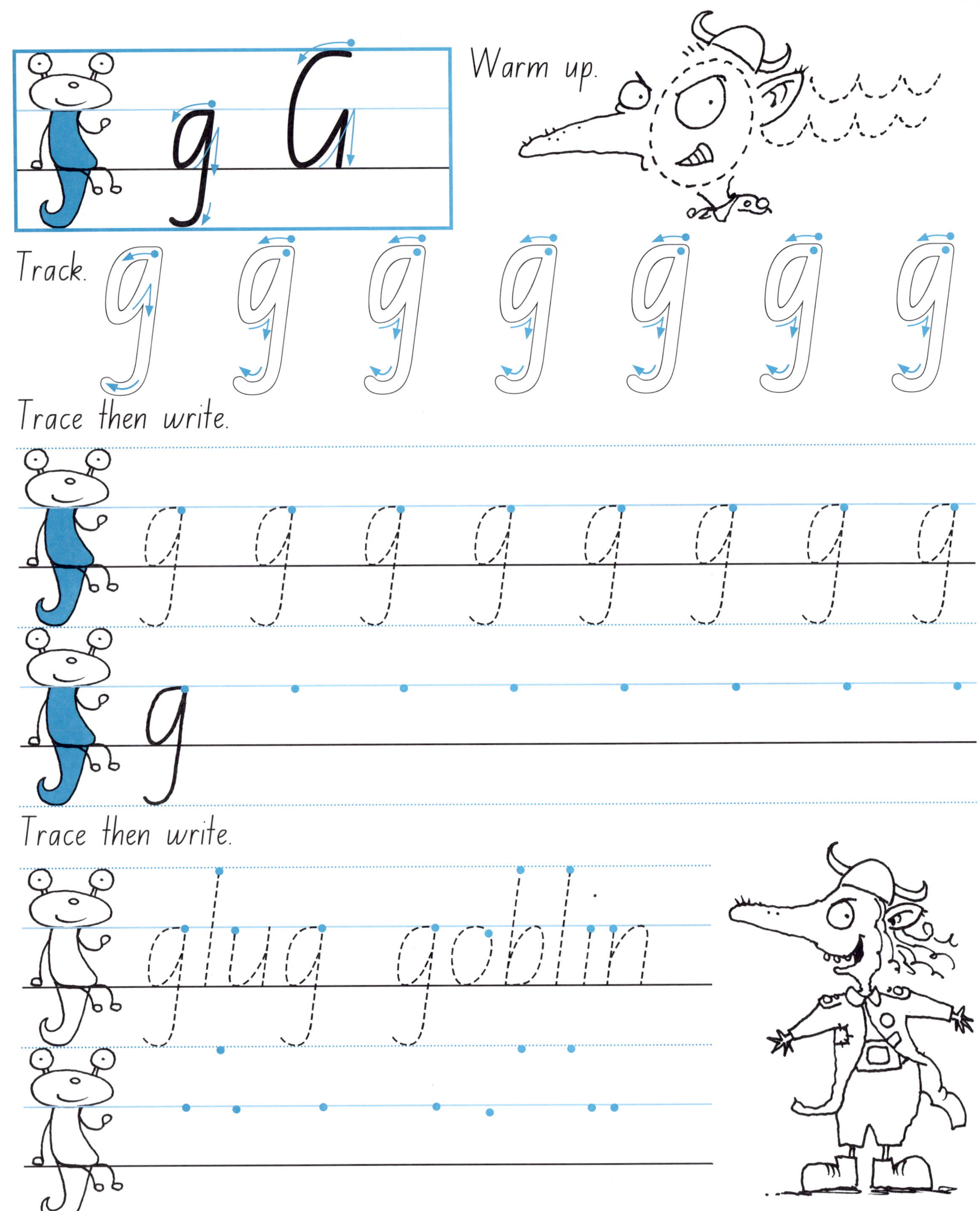

Handwriting: anticlockwise ellipse, long letter (g).
Grammar: commands, proper noun (Gruff).
Punctuation: quoted speech, quotation marks, exclamation mark.
Spelling and vocabulary: game, gasp, get, glue, go, goat, goblin, going, gone, grandma, grandpa, grape, grip.
Literary elements: alliteration, folk tales (The Three Billy Goats Gruff), story characters (goblin), onomatopoeia (glug).

Trace then write.

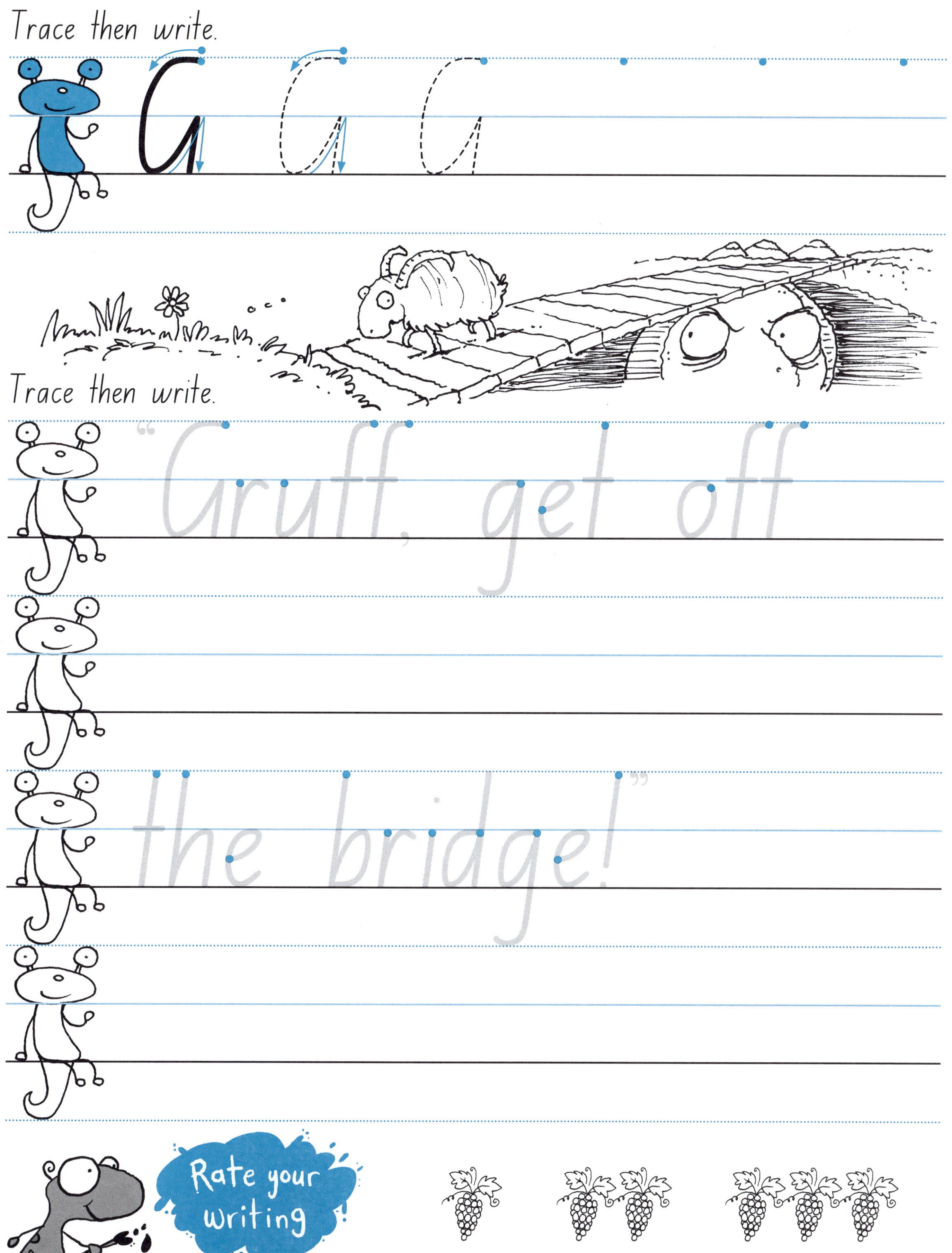

Trace then write.

q Q

Warm up.

Track.

Trace then write.

q

Trace then write.

quoll quit quick

Handwriting: anticlockwise ellipse, long letter (q).
Grammar: simple sentence, proper noun (Queenie), adjective (quick).
Punctuation: upper-case letters to start a sentence, full stop.
Spelling and vocabulary: equal, quail, queen, quick, quiet, quit, quite, quiz, quoll.
Literary elements: alliteration.

Trace then write.

Q Q Q

Trace then write.

Queenie is

quite quick.

Rate your writing

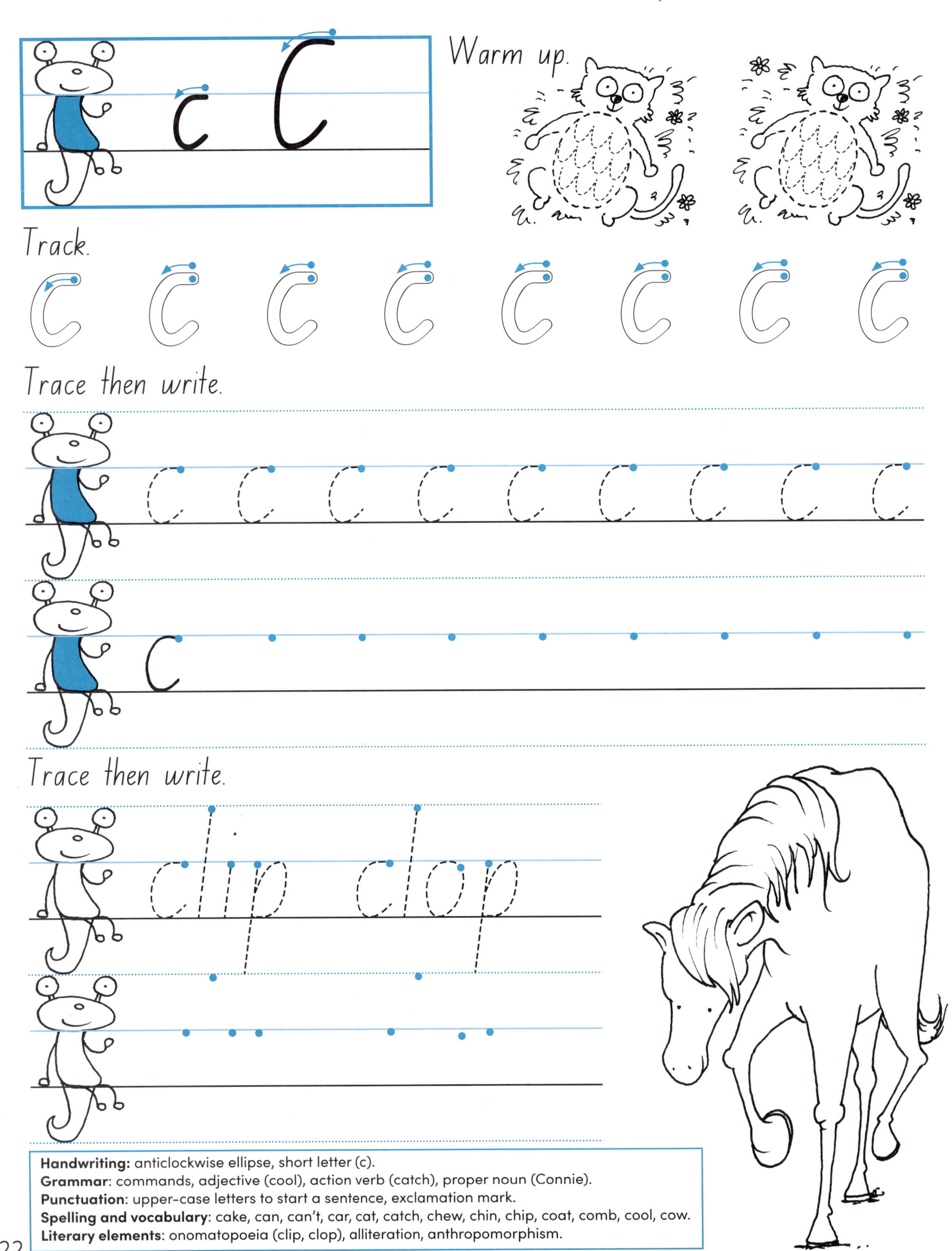

Handwriting: anticlockwise ellipse, short letter (c).
Grammar: commands, adjective (cool), action verb (catch), proper noun (Connie).
Punctuation: upper-case letters to start a sentence, exclamation mark.
Spelling and vocabulary: cake, can, can't, car, cat, catch, chew, chin, chip, coat, comb, cool, cow.
Literary elements: onomatopoeia (clip, clop), alliteration, anthropomorphism.

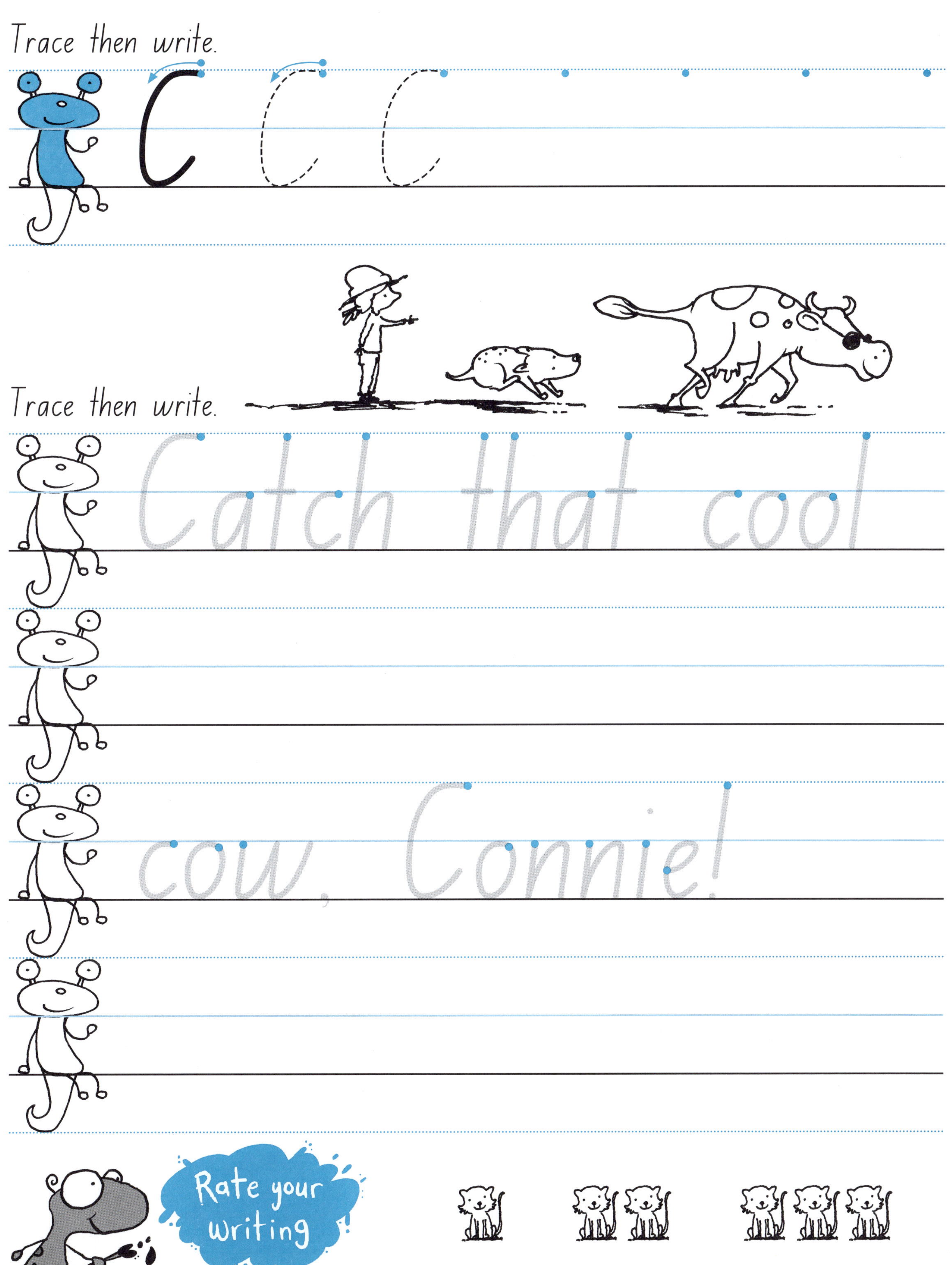
Trace then write.
C
Trace then write.
Catch that cool
cow, Connie!
Rate your writing

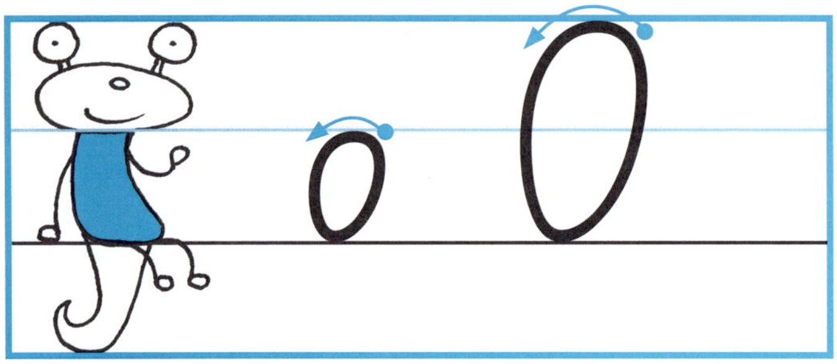

o O

Warm up.

Track.

Trace then write.

Trace then write.

Handwriting: anticlockwise ellipse, short letter (o).
Grammar: simple sentence, statement.
Punctuation: upper-case letters to start a sentence, full stop.
Spelling and vocabulary: October, often, once, one, only, open, orange, oven, owl, ox.
Literary elements: alliteration, story characters (ogre).

Trace then write.

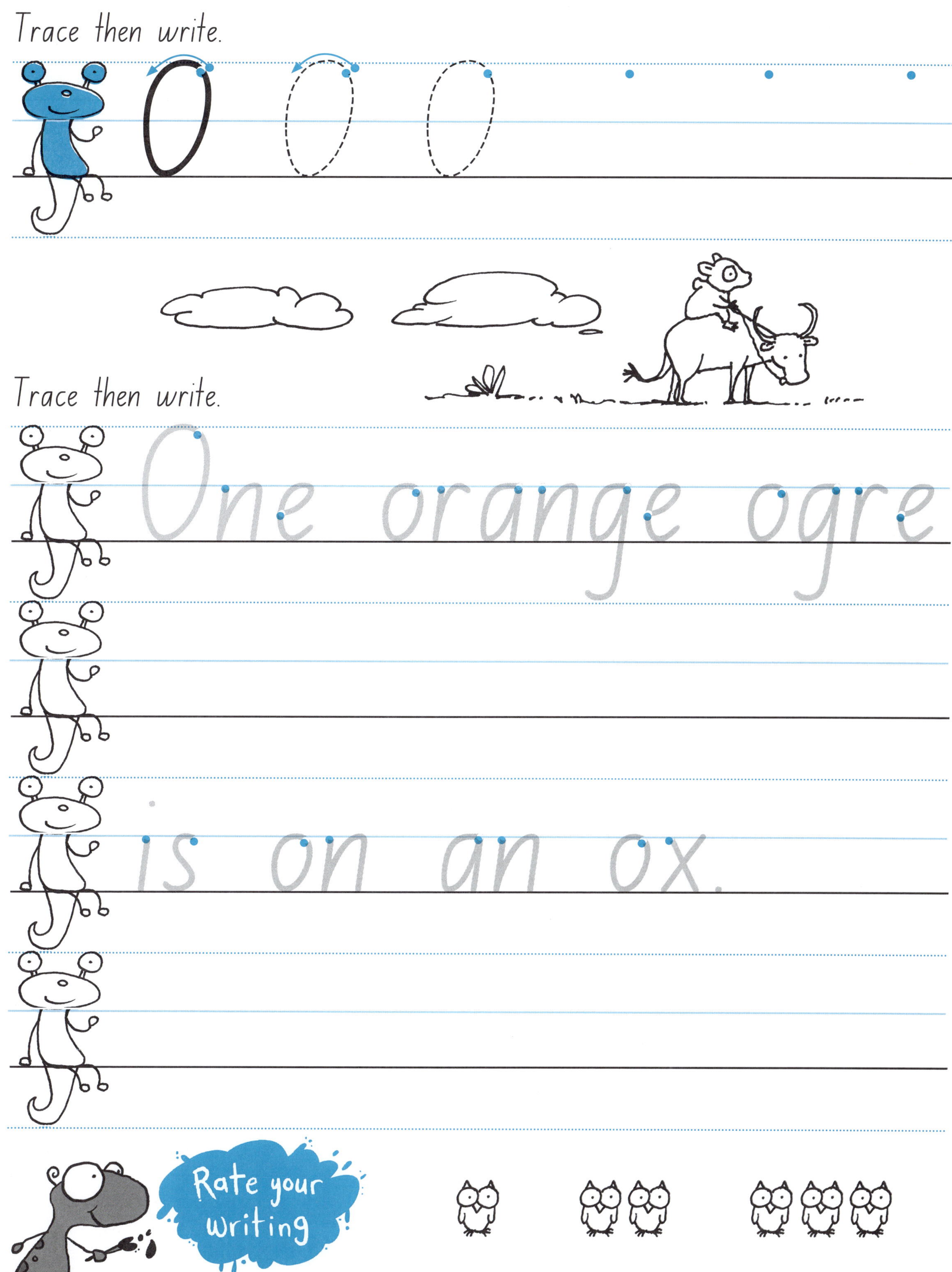

Trace then write.

Handwriting: anticlockwise ellipse, short letter (s).
Grammar: simple sentence, statement, proper noun (Samson), action verb (sat), saying verb (said).
Punctuation: upper-case letters to start a sentence, full stop.
Spelling and vocabulary: said, sand, Saturday, saw, see, send, September, seven, sister, six, slump, snail, snort, spider, squid.
Literary elements: alliteration, onomatopoeia (snort).

Trace then write.

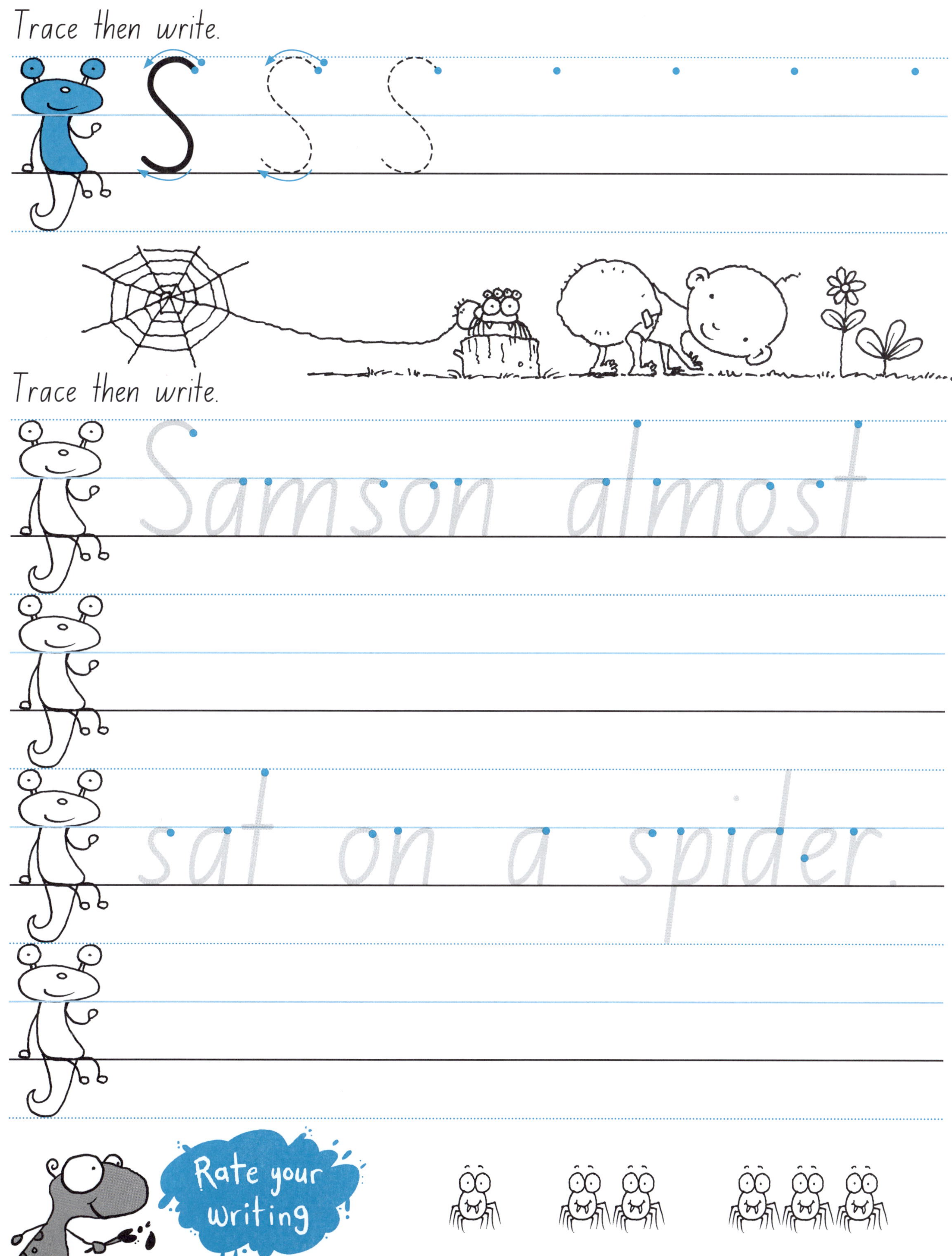

Trace then write.

Samson almost

sat on a spider.

Rate your writing

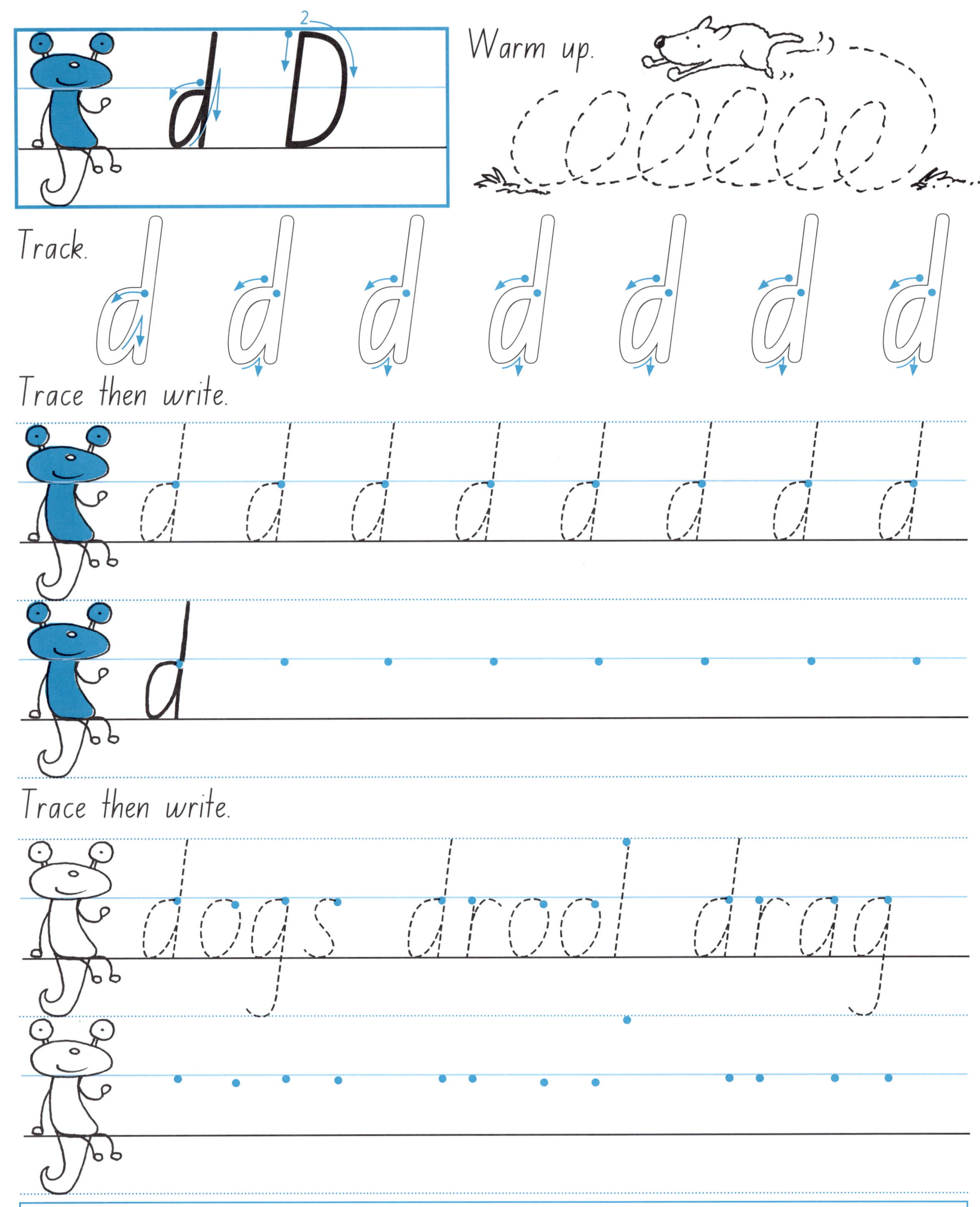

Handwriting: anticlockwise ellipse, tall letter (d).
Grammar: simple sentence, statement, proper noun (Daisy).
Punctuation: upper-case letters to start a sentence, full stop.
Spelling and vocabulary: dance, December, did, disco, do, dog, done, door, drab, drag, drip, drool, drop, drum, doll, duck.
Literary elements: alliteration, anthropomorphism.

Trace then write.

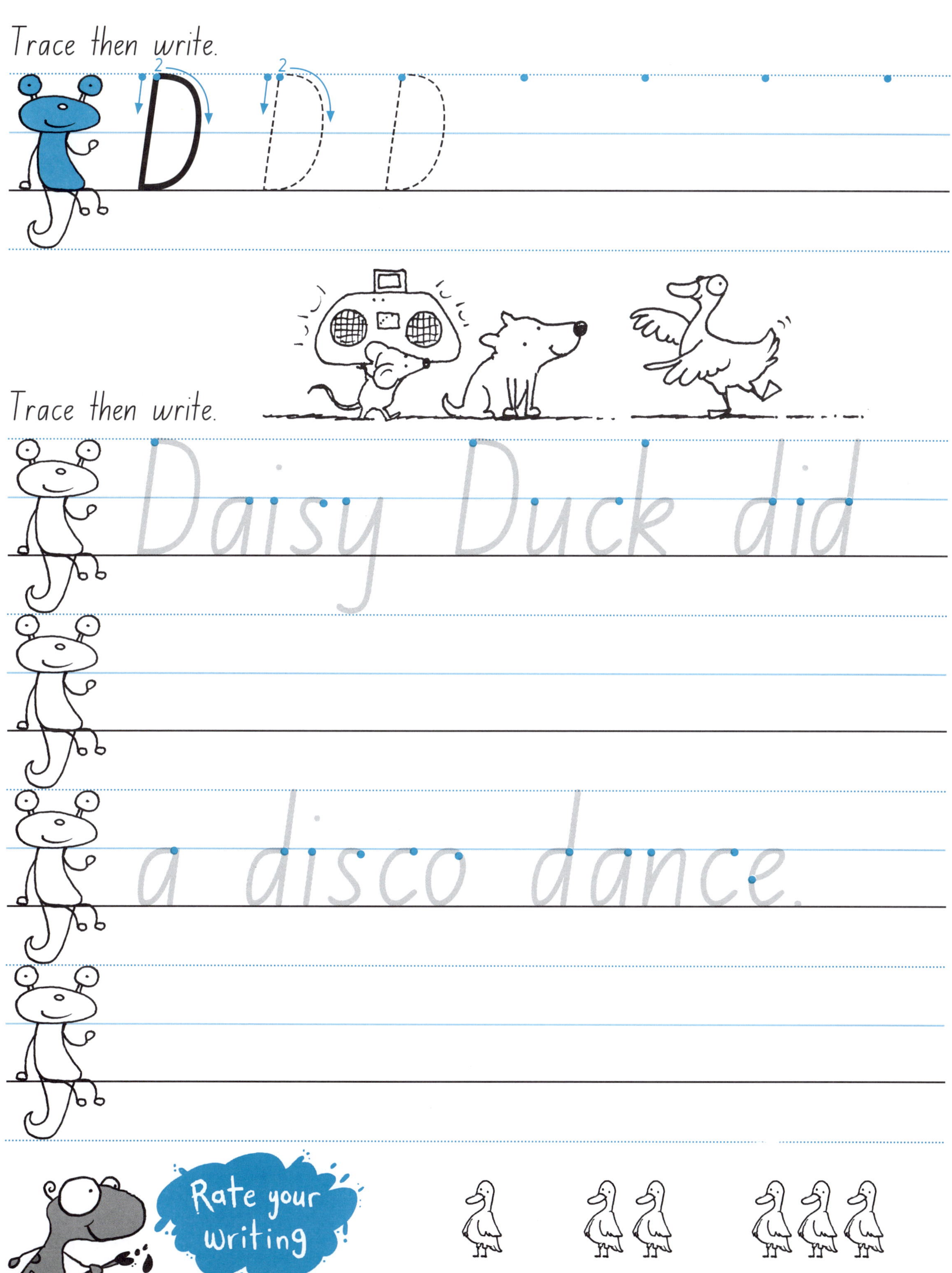

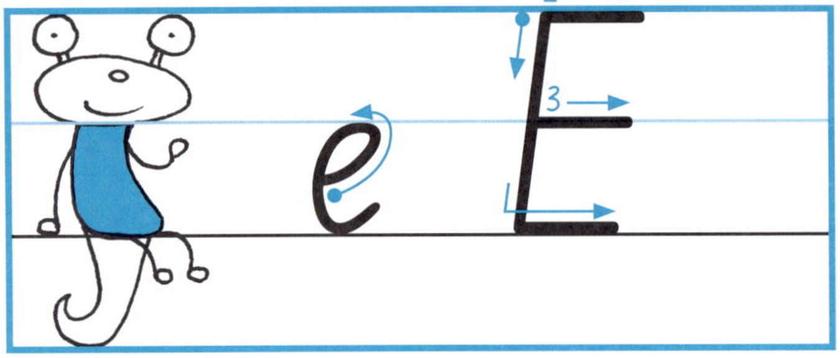

e E

Warm up.

Track.

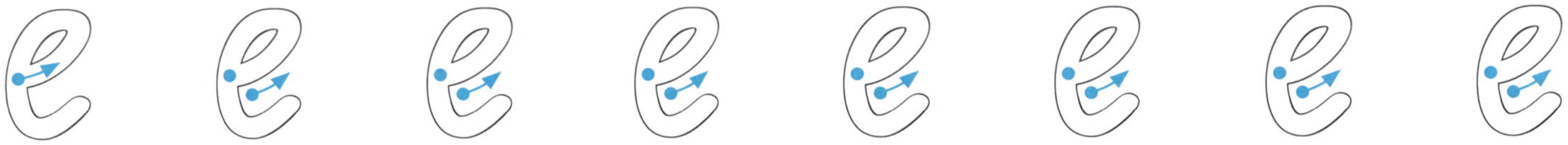

Trace then write.

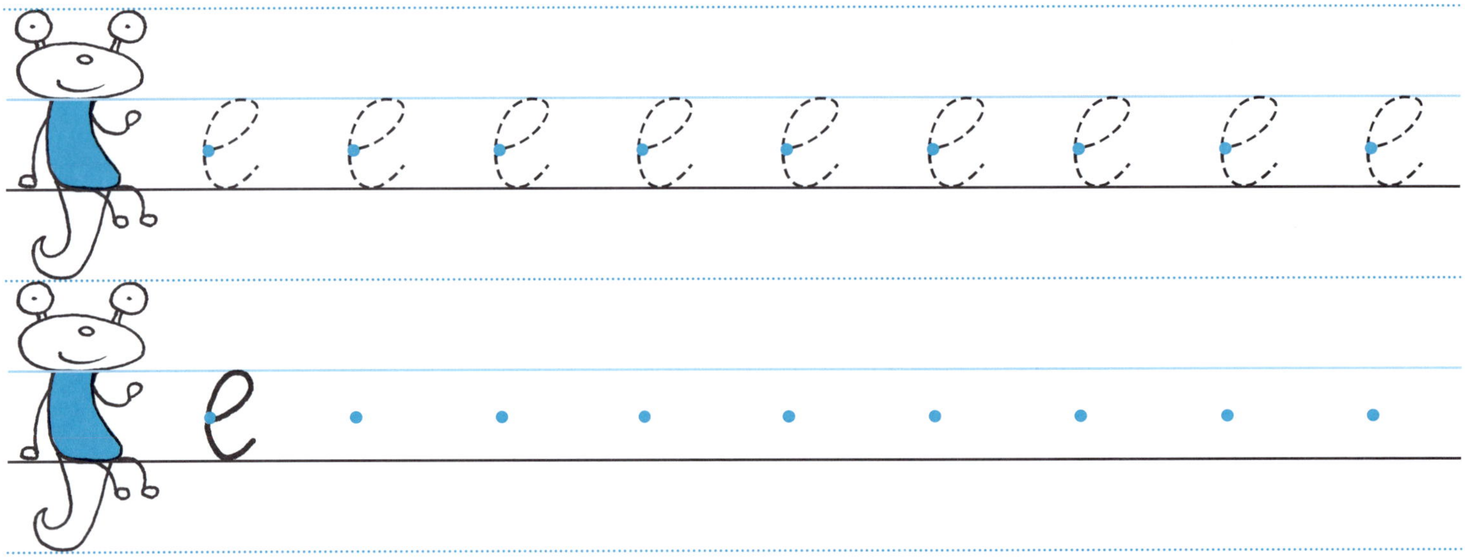

e

Trace then write.

every elephant

Handwriting: anticlockwise ellipse, short letter (e).
Grammar: simple sentence, saying verb (yelled).
Punctuation: upper-case letters to start a sentence, exclamation mark, quotation marks.
Spelling and vocabulary: eagle, ear, earth, eat, eating, egg, elephant, elf, even, every, extra.
Literary elements: alliteration, story characters (elf), onomatopoeia (eek).

Trace then write.
E
Eek!
Trace then write.
"Eek! An eagle!"
yelled the elf.
Rate your writing

Handwriting: clockwise ellipse, short letter (n).
Grammar: simple sentence, adverb that tells how (noisily), action verb (nibbled), proper noun (Nonna).
Punctuation: upper-case letters to start a sentence, full stop.
Spelling and vocabulary: name, nest, new, newt, next, nibble, nice, nine, no, noodle, not, never, Nonna, November, now.
Literary elements: alliteration.

Trace then write.

N N N

Trace then write.

Nonna noisily

nibbled noodles.

Rate your writing

Handwriting: clockwise ellipse, short letter (r).
Grammar: simple sentence, adjectives (rude).
Punctuation: upper-case letters to start a sentence, full stop.
Spelling and vocabulary: rabbit, raft, ran, rang, rat, read, real, red, reek, ring, roast, robot, rot, rude, run, rush, rushing.
Literary elements: alliteration.

Trace then write.

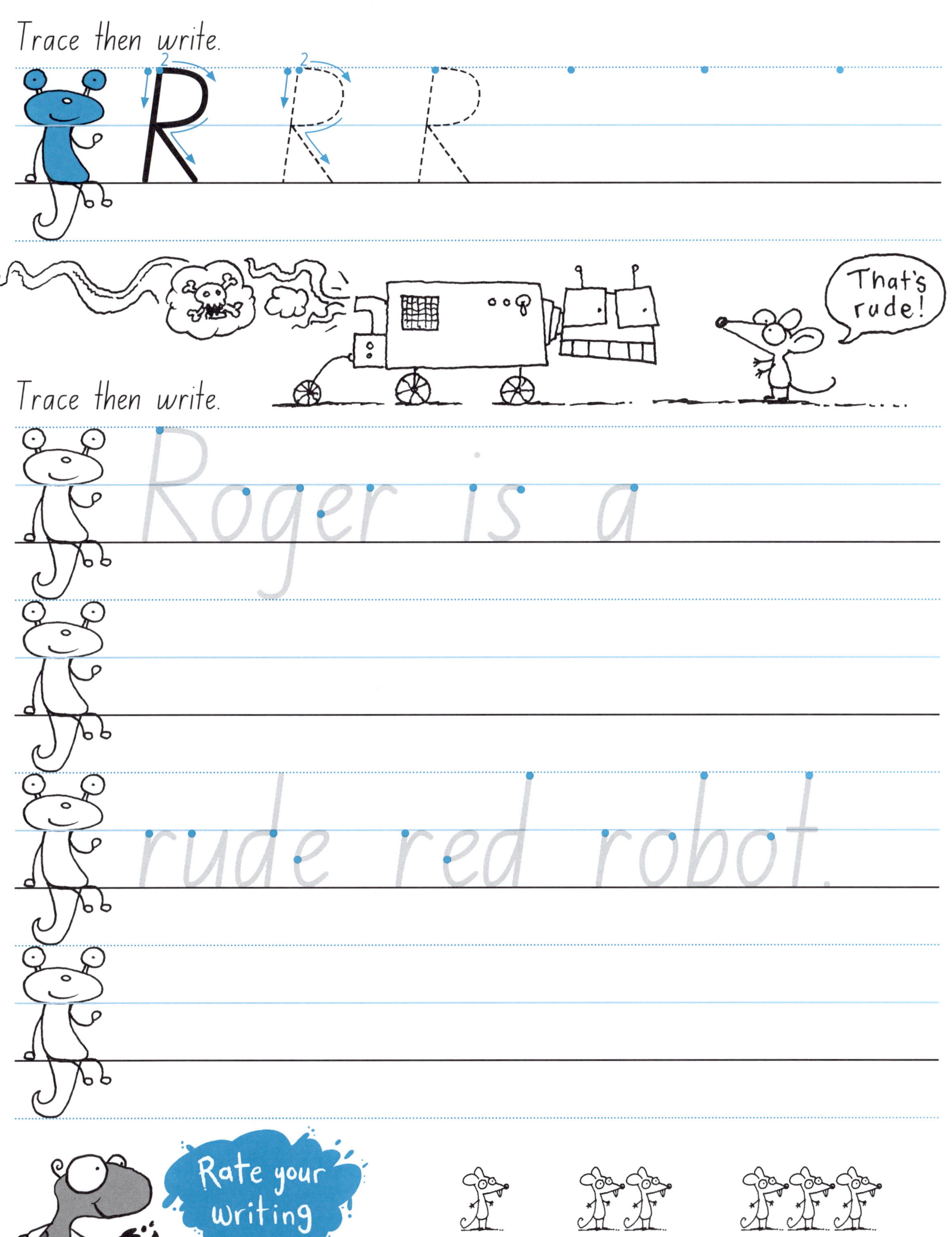

Handwriting: clockwise ellipse, short letter (m).
Grammar: simple sentence, action verb (munch).
Punctuation: upper-case letters to start a sentence, full stop.
Spelling and vocabulary: mad, March, May, melon, meow, merry, mess, Monday, monkey, monster, moo, mother, mud, mum, munch.
Literary elements: alliteration.

Trace then write.

M M M

Trace then write.

Merry monkeys

munch on melons.

Rate your writing

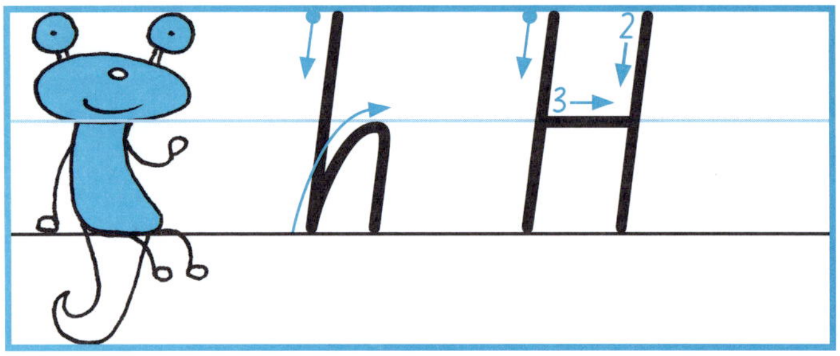

h H

Warm up.

Track.

h h h h h h h

Trace then write.

h h h h h h h h

h

Trace then write.

howl hiss hum

Handwriting: clockwise ellipse, tall letter (h).
Grammar: saying verb (shouted), adjective (hungry), proper noun (Hansel).
Punctuation: upper-case letters to start a sentence, quoted speech, exclamation mark, quotation marks.
Spelling and vocabulary: hair, hang, hawk, hen, hid, hide, hiss, hum, hog, home, honey, hospital, howl, hungry, heart.
Literary elements: alliteration, onomatopoeia (hiss, howl), folk tales (Hansel and Gretel).

Trace then write.

H H H

Trace then write.

"Hello!" shouted

hungry Hansel.

Rate your writing

k K

Warm up.

Track.

k k k k k k k

Trace then write.

k k k k k k k k

k

Trace then write.

Handwriting: clockwise ellipse, tall letter (k).
Grammar: simple sentence, proper noun (King Kong).
Punctuation: upper-case letters to start a sentence, full stop.
Spelling and vocabulary: key, kind, kiss, kitten, koala, silent k (knee, knew, knit, knot, know).
Literary elements: alliteration, story characters (King Kong), anthropomorphism.

Trace then write.

K K K

Trace then write.

King Kong

kept knitting.

Rate your writing

Handwriting: clockwise ellipse, tall letter (b). **Grammar**: simple sentence, action verb (boogied).
Punctuation: upper-case letters to start a sentence, full stop.
Spelling and vocabulary: baby, bag, banana, band, bang, bunyip, before, best, better, big, bird, boat, book, brag, bring, brown, burp. The word "bunyip" is from the Wathawurung and Dharug languages.
Literary elements: alliteration, onomatopoeia (beep), anthropomorphism.

Trace then write.

Handwriting: clockwise ellipse, long letter (p).
Grammar: simple sentence/statement, action verbs (poked, plod), proper noun (Pedro).
Punctuation: upper-case letters to start a sentence, full stop.
Spelling and vocabulary: peep, pet, pencil, pig, pimple, pink, plop, plus, poke, pong, pony, possum, post, pumpkin, push, put, python.
Literary elements: alliteration, onomatopoeia (plop).

Trace then write.

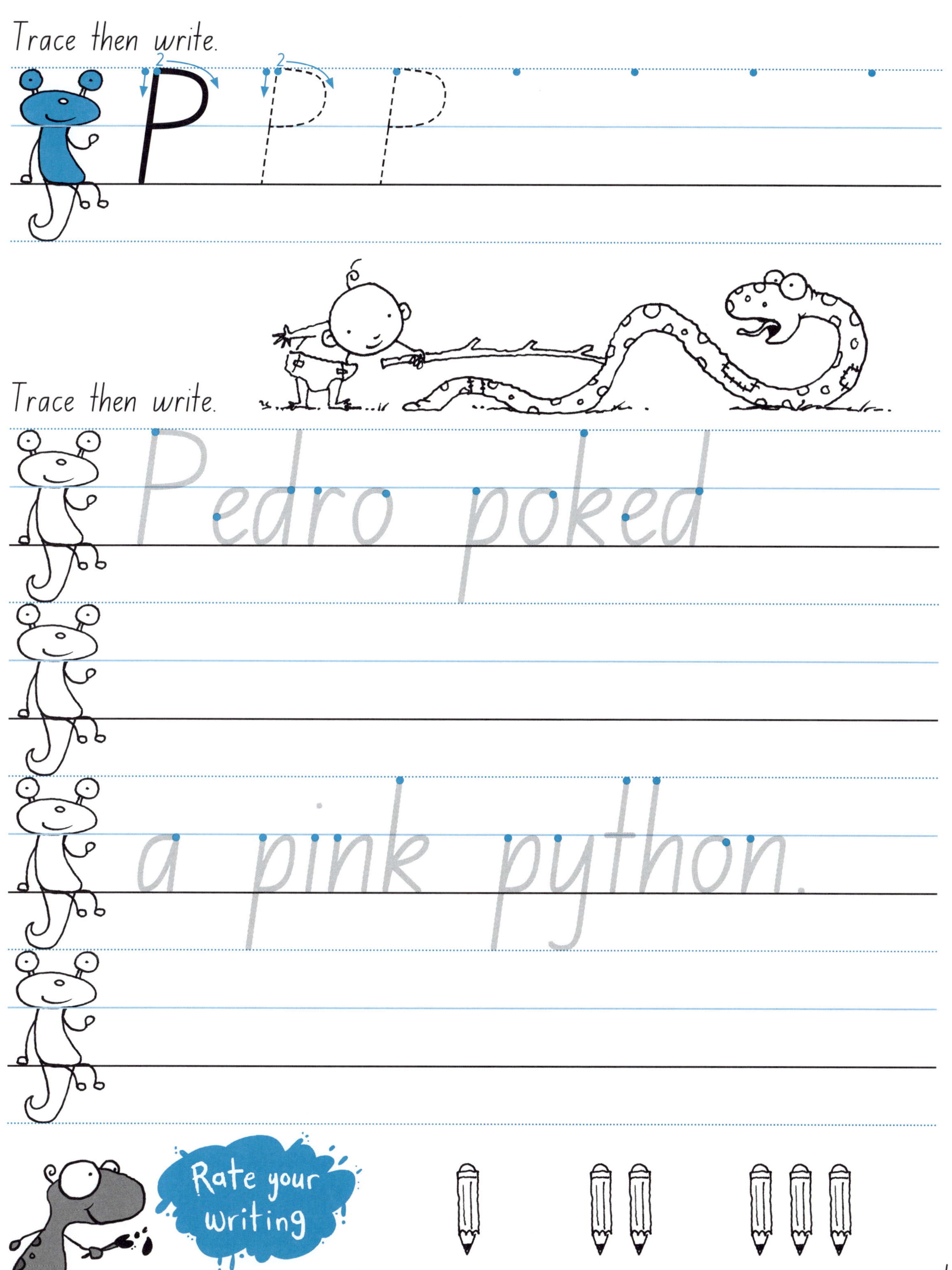

Handwriting: downward diagonal stroke, tall letter (l).
Grammar: simple sentence/statement, proper noun (Lilly), adjective (lovely), action verbs (limp, lick, leap).
Punctuation: upper-case letters to start a sentence, full stop.
Spelling and vocabulary: lazy, leap, left, lesson, lick, life, lift, limb, limp, lion, list, live, lizard, llama, log, lose, lost, love, lovely, lumpy.
Literary elements: alliteration.

Trace then write.

L L L

Trace then write.

Little Lilly loves

lovely llamas.

Rate your writing

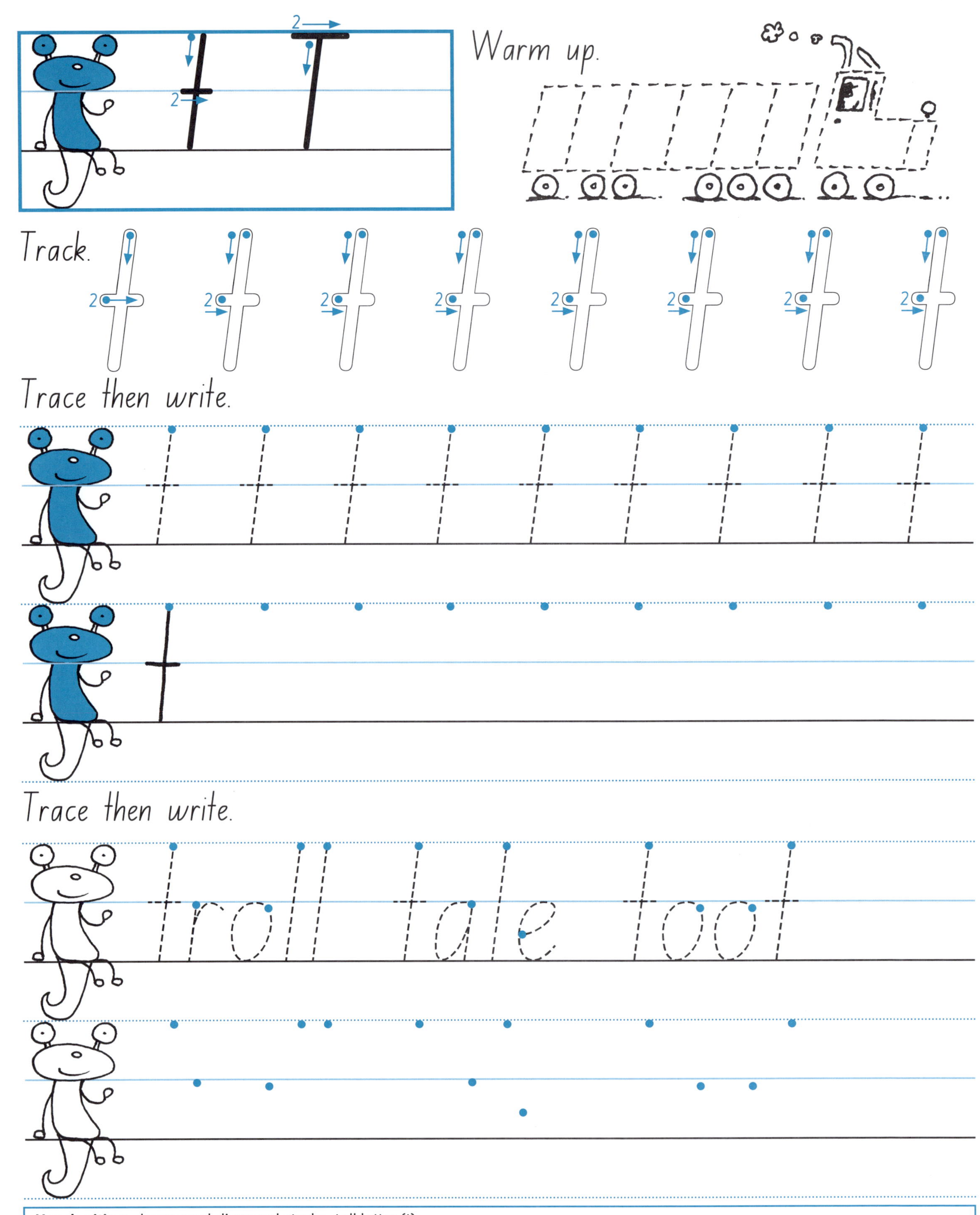

Handwriting: downward diagonal stroke, tall letter (t).
Grammar: simple sentence/statement.
Punctuation: upper-case letters to start a sentence, full stop.
Spelling and vocabulary: tale, take, teeth, tell, Tuesday, Thursday, time, timid, took, toot, tooth, trap, try, turtle, ten, three, twelve, two.
Literary elements: alliteration, story characters (troll), onomatopoeia (toot), play on words (took its time).

Trace then write.

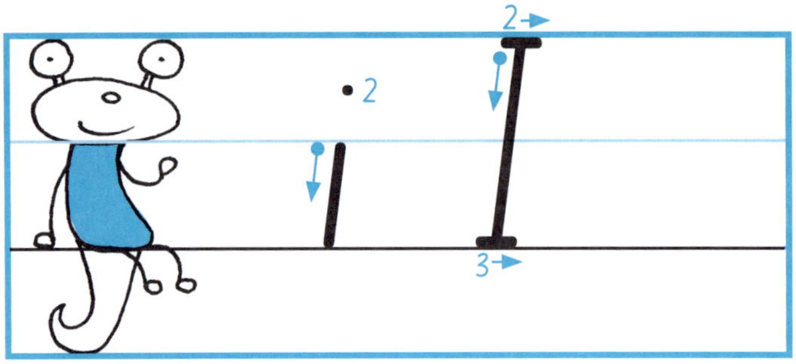

i I

•2

2→

3→

Warm up.

Track.

2 2 2 2 2 2 2 2 2

Trace then write.

i i i i i i i i i i i

i

Trace then write.

itchy iguana ink

Handwriting: downward diagonal stroke, short letter (i).
Grammar: simple sentence/statement, proper noun (Iggy), adjective (itchy).
Punctuation: upper-case letters to start a sentence, full stop.
Spelling and vocabulary: icky, idea, idol, igloo, iguana, imp, in, ink, insect, inside, into, is, isn't, it, itchy.
Literary elements: alliteration.

Trace then write.

Trace then write.

Handwriting: downward diagonal stroke, long letter (j).
Grammar: simple sentence/statement, action verbs (jiggles, jumps, jog), proper noun (Jill).
Punctuation: upper-case letters to start a sentence, full stop.
Spelling and vocabulary: jagged, jam, jammed, January, jet, jelly bean, jiggle, joey, jog, join, joke, July, June, jump, just.
Literary elements: alliteration, nursery rhyme (Jack and Jill went up the hill).

Trace then write.

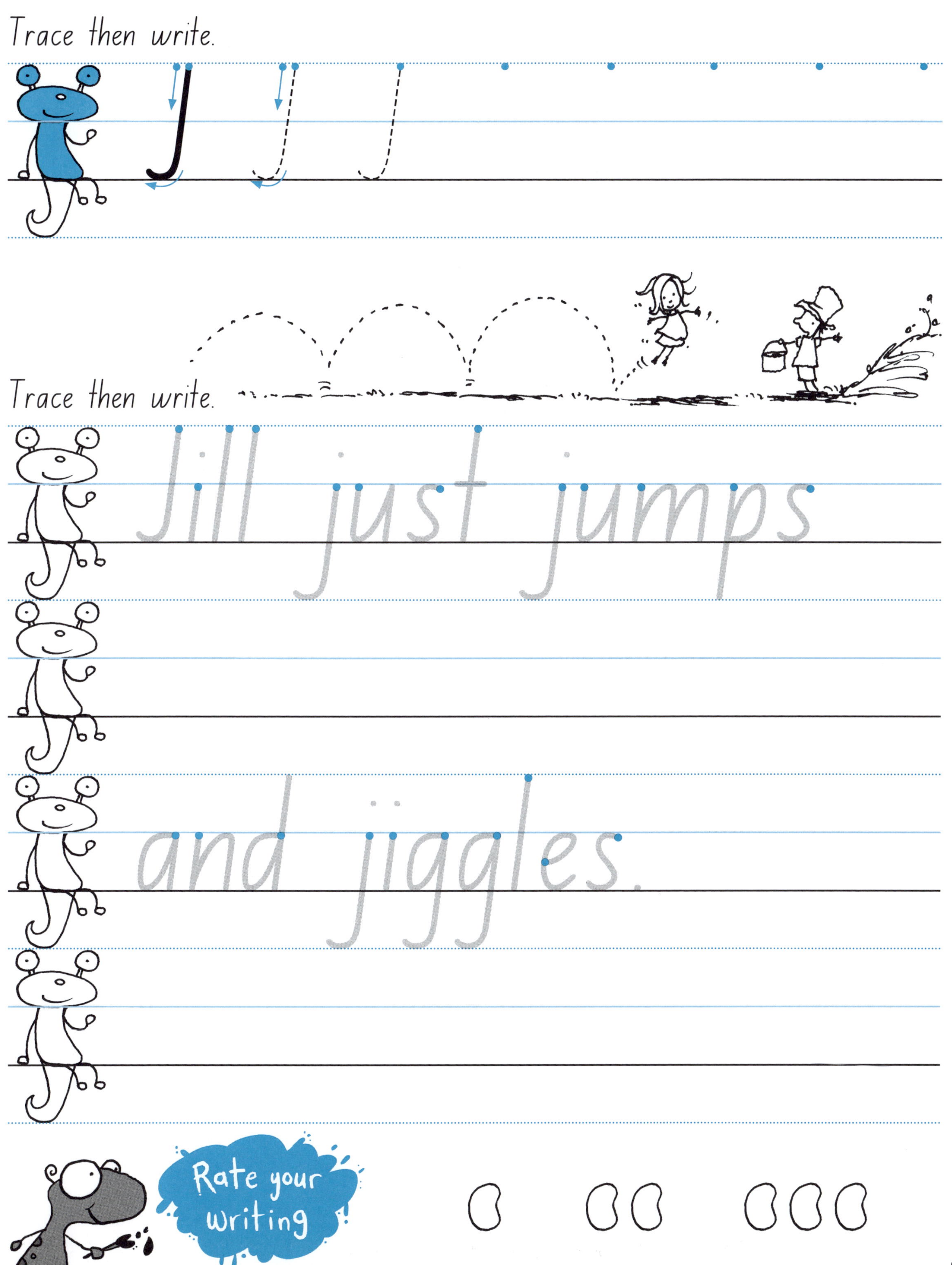

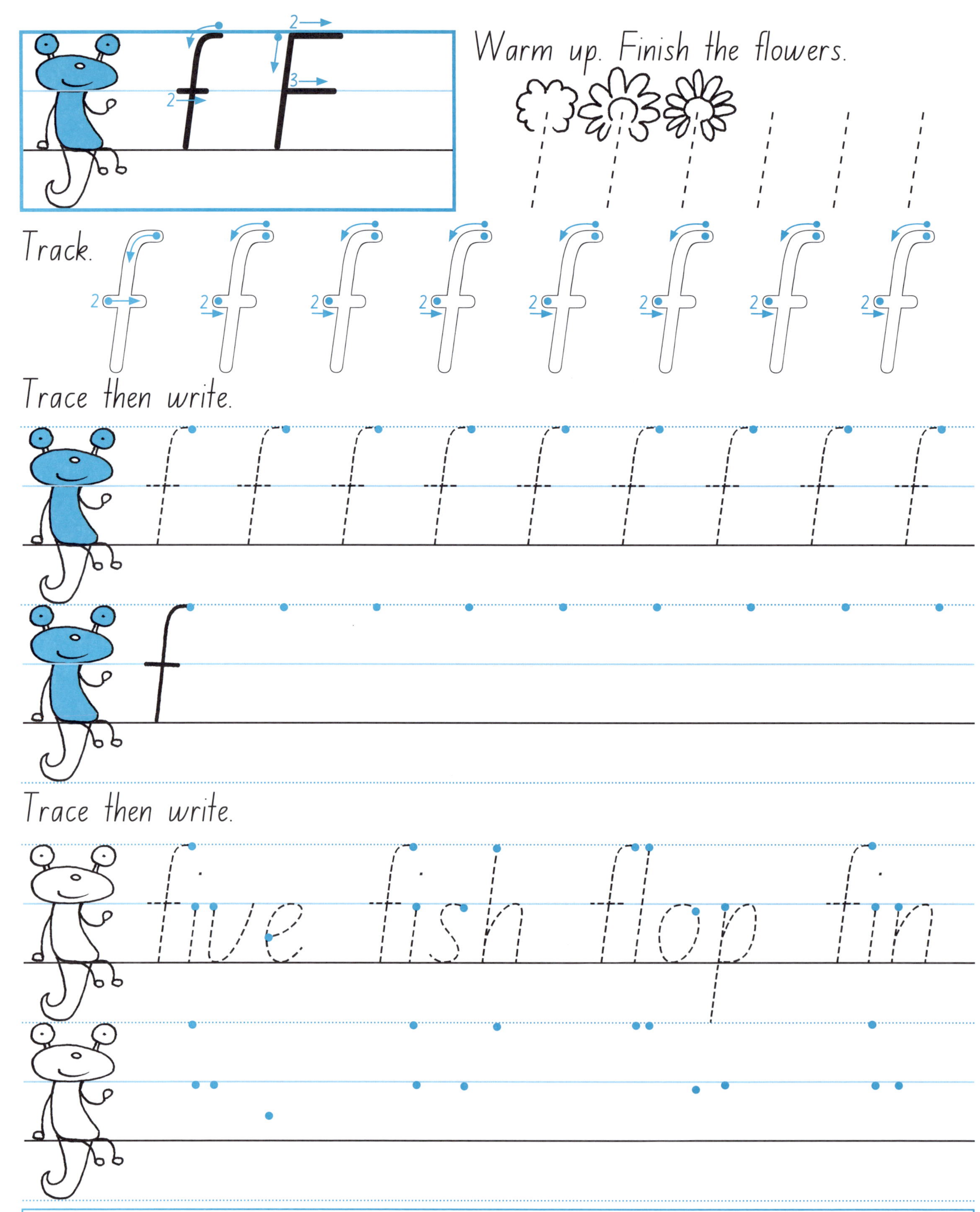

Handwriting: downward diagonal stroke, tall letter (f).
Grammar: simple sentence, proper noun (Felix), adjective (fast), action verb (fled).
Punctuation: upper-case letters to start a sentence, full stop.
Spelling and vocabulary: fast, February, feel, fin, find, first, fish, fit, five, fleck, fled, flesh, flop, foam, foot, Friday, frisky, fry, fun.
Literary elements: alliteration.

Trace then write.

Trace then write.

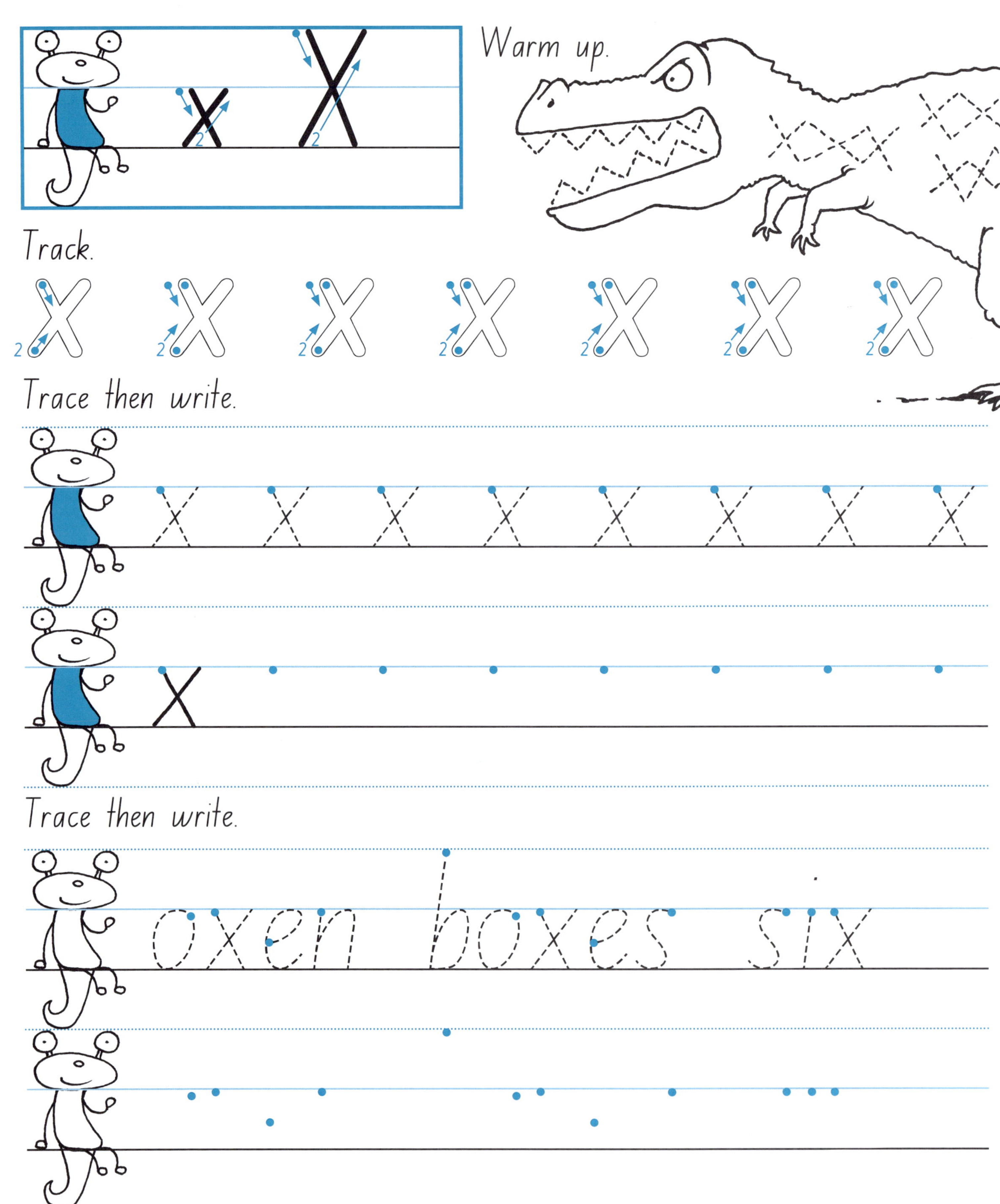

Handwriting: downward diagonal stroke, short letter (x).
Grammar: simple sentence, statement.
Punctuation: upper-case letters to start a sentence, full stop.
Spelling and vocabulary: apostrophe (don't), box, exam, fox, mix, oxen, six, T-Rex, taxi, text, wax, X-ray, xylophone.

Trace then write.

X X X

Trace then write.

Xylophones don't

mix with foxes.

Rate your writing

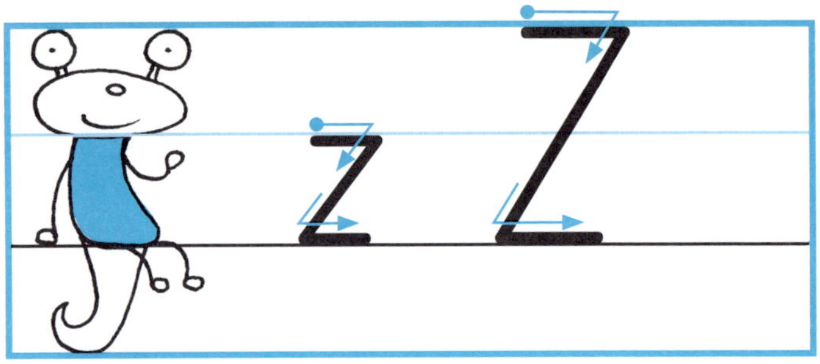

z Z

Warm up.

Track.

Z Z Z Z Z Z Z Z

Trace then write.

z z z z z z z z

z

Trace then write.

zebra whiz zoo

Handwriting: downward diagonal stroke, short letter (z).
Grammar: simple sentence/statement, proper noun (Zoe), possessive apostrophe (Zoe's).
Punctuation: upper-case letters to start a sentence, full stop.
Spelling and vocabulary: doze, quiz, zany, zap, zebra, zero, zest, zesty, zing, zip, zoo.
Literary elements: alliteration, onomatopoeia (whiz, zip, zap).

Trace then write.

Trace then write.

Trace then write.

11 eleven

12 twelve

13 thirteen

14 fourteen

15 fifteen

Rate your writing

☆ ☆☆ ☆☆☆

Trace then write.

16 sixteen

17 seventeen

18 eighteen

19 nineteen

20 twenty

Rate your writing

☆ ☆☆ ☆☆☆

Trace then write.

10 ten

20 twenty

30 thirty

40 forty

50 fifty

Rate your writing

☆ ☆☆ ☆☆☆

Trace then write.

60 sixty

In dog years, she's the same age as me.

70 seventy

80 eighty

90 ninety

100 one hundred

Rate your writing

☆ ☆☆ ☆☆☆

Trace then write.

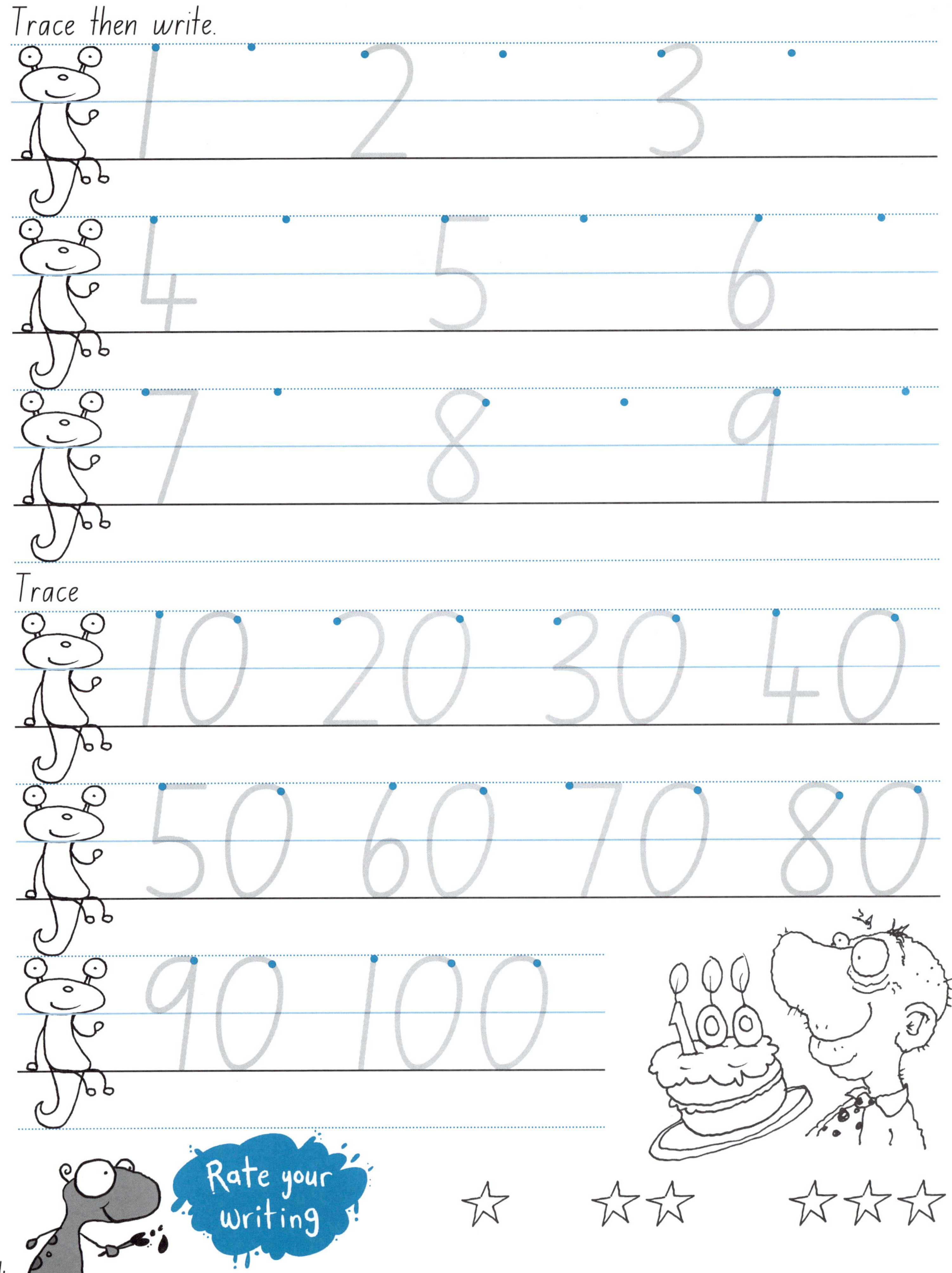